Kids First Cookbook: Learning to Cook is Fun

Speedy Publishing LLC
40 E. Main St. #1156
Newark, DE 19711

www.speedypublishing.com

Copyright 2015
9781681453880
First Printed February 6, 2015

 speedypublishing

Cooking Tips for kids:

1. Always wash and dry your hands thoroughly before cooking.

2. Check all the listed ingredients - get them out ready to start cooking.

3. Wash all vegetables and fruit before you use them.

4. Make sure you have all the right sized pans, baking tins and other containers needed.

5. Set the oven to the required temperature and preheat.

6. Get a grown up to help you with tricky recipes involving sharp knives and hot surfaces.

7. Always wear oven gloves when using hot pans, baking trays.

8. Clean utensils and scrub cutting boards after use. Use a different cutting board for raw and cooked food.

9. Taste food before you add any salt - it may not need it.

10. Experiment with different herbs and spices, these make food delicious without the flavour of fat and salt.

Breakfast

Banana Bread

Ingredients:

1 2/3 cups all-purpose flour
2 teaspoons baking powder
1/2 teaspoon salt
1/4 teaspoon baking soda
3 medium very ripe bananas, peeled
2/3 cup sugar
1/3 cup vegetable oil
2 eggs
1 1/2 teaspoons vanilla extract

Directions:

Before you start
Be sure an adult is nearby to help.

Preheat an oven to 350°F. Grease an 8 1/2-by-4 1/2-inch metal loaf pan with butter.

Make the batter
In a bowl, using a wooden spoon, stir together the flour, baking powder, salt and baking soda.

In a large bowl, smash the bananas with a fork. Add the sugar, oil, eggs and vanilla and beat with the wooden spoon until well blended.

Add the flour mixture to the banana mixture and stir just until blended.

Bake the bread

Scrape the batter into the prepared pan, spreading it evenly with the wooden spoon. Put the pan in the oven and bake until a toothpick inserted into the center of the bread comes out with just a few crumbs clinging to it, about 45 minutes.

Using oven mitts, remove the pan from the oven, set it on a wire cooling rack and let cool for 20 minutes.

Remove the bread from the pan

Gently run a table knife along the inside edge of the pan to loosen the bread from the sides.

Using oven mitts, turn the pan on its side and slip the loaf out onto the wire rack. Let the loaf cool for 15 minutes before serving. Makes 1 loaf.

Banana Pancakes

Ingredients:

6 tablespoons (3/4 stick) unsalted butter

1 1/2 cups all-purpose flour

2 tablespoons sugar

2 1/2 teaspoons baking powder

1/4 teaspoon salt

1 small, very ripe banana, peeled

1 cup milk

2 eggs

1/2 teaspoon vanilla extract

Maple syrup for serving

Sliced bananas for serving

Directions:

Be sure an adult is nearby to help.

Cut the butter into 3 equal pieces. Put 2 of the butter pieces in a small saucepan and set the remaining piece aside. Set the pan over medium heat and stir with a wooden spoon until melted, 1 to 2 minutes. Using a pot holder, remove the pan from the heat and set it aside to cool.

In a bowl, combine the flour, sugar, baking powder and salt. Mix with a fork until well blended.

Put the banana in a small bowl. Mash with a fork until almost smooth. Add the milk, eggs and vanilla and stir with the fork until well blended. Pour the banana mixture and the melted butter into the flour mixture. Mix gently with a rubber spatula until the batter is just blended. The batter should still be a little bit lumpy.

Put a griddle over medium heat until hot. To test if the griddle is hot enough, flick a drop of water onto it. It is ready if the drop dances quickly and evaporates. Put half of the remaining butter onto the griddle and spread it with a metal spatula. Drop the batter by 1/4 cupfuls onto the griddle, spacing them about 3 inches apart.

Cook until a few holes form on top of each pancake and the underside is golden brown, about 2 minutes. Carefully slide the metal spatula under each pancake and turn it over. Cook until the bottom is golden brown and the top is puffed, 1 to 2 minutes more. Using the spatula, transfer the pancakes to a serving plate.

Repeat with the remaining batter. Serve the pancakes while still hot with maple syrup and sliced bananas. Makes twelve 4-inch pancakes.

Cheese and Herb Omelette

Ingredients:

2 tablespoons cream cheese, at room temperature
1 tablespoon chopped fresh chives, thyme, basil or parsley
2 eggs
1 tablespoon water
Pinch of salt
Pinch of freshly ground pepper
1 tablespoon unsalted butter

Directions:

Be sure an adult is nearby to help.

In a small bowl, combine the cream cheese and herbs. Mash with a table fork until blended. Set aside.

In another small bowl, combine the eggs, water, salt and pepper. Using a clean table fork, mix together until just blended. The eggs should not be foamy.

Put the butter in a small nonstick fry pan and set over medium heat. When the butter is melted and starts to foam, swirl the pan to coat the bottom with the butter. Pour the eggs into the pan and cook until the edges begin to look set, about 45 seconds. Holding the pan steady with a pot holder, use a spatula to lift up an edge of the omelette and tilt the pan slightly toward that edge. The uncooked egg in the center will run onto the pan bottom. Continue to cook and repeat the lift-and-tilt movement 2 more times at other points around the edge.

When the center of the omelette no longer looks runny but is still moist, drop teaspoonfuls of the cream cheese mixture over half of the omelette. Slide the spatula under the other half of the omelette and flip it over the cream cheese half.

Gripping the pan handle firmly with the pot holder, hold the pan over a serving plate. Tilt the pan slightly and let the omelette slide out of it onto the plate. Serve immediately. Serves 1.

Fruity Morning Shakes

Ingredients:

1 container (8 ounces) vanilla yogurt

6 strawberries, stems cut off, or 1 small ripe peach, pit removed and cut into chunks, or 1 cup blueberries

Ice cubes (optional)

Directions:

Be sure an adult is nearby to help.

Put the yogurt and sugar in the container of an electric blender. Add your choice of fruit.

Put the yogurt in the container of an electric blender. Make sure it is on tight! Hold down the lid with your hand (so the lid is not forced off by the spinning liquid) and turn the blender on to high speed. Blend until the shake is thick and smooth.

Fill 1 or 2 glasses with ice cubes, if you want your shake frostier, and pour the shake into the glass(es). Serve immediately. Serves 1 or 2.

Lunch

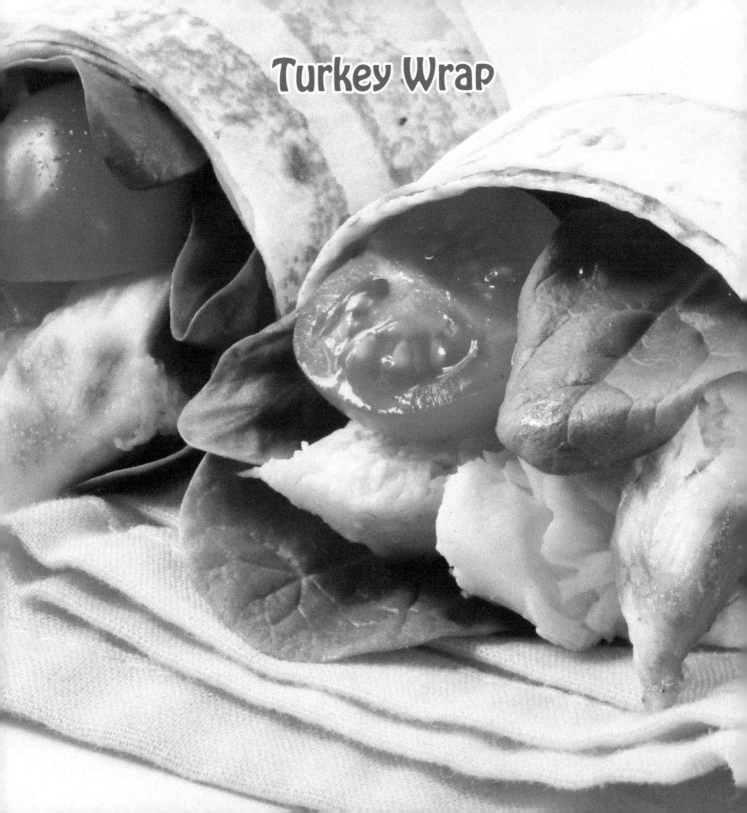
Turkey Wrap

Ingredients:

- 1/3 English cucumber
- 1 sheet lavash bread
- 1 tablespoon cream cheese, at room temperature
- 4 fresh basil leaves
- 2 or 3 slices turkey
- 4 fresh spinach leaves

Directions:

Slice the cucumber
Before you start, be sure an adult is nearby to help.

Put the cucumber on a cutting board. Using a sharp knife, cut off the ends. Slice the cucumber into rounds as thin as possible.

Spread the bread
Put the lavash bread on the cutting board. Using the sharp knife, trim the edges to make a neat, 8-inch square.

Using a butter knife, spread the cream cheese over the lavash, leaving a 1-inch-wide border uncovered around the edges.

Layer the fillings

Layer the sliced cucumber on top of the cream cheese.
Top the cucumber with a layer of the basil leaves.
Continue the layering, first with the turkey and then
with the spinach leaves.

Roll the wrap

Starting from the edge closest to you, roll up the
lavash into a tube. Using the sharp knife, cut the roll
in half on the diagonal. Serve immediately. Makes 1
sandwich.

Cheese Quesadilla

Ingredients:

2 flour tortillas, each 8 inches
1 teaspoon olive oil or vegetable oil
1/2 cup shredded Monterey jack cheese
2 tablespoons prepared salsa
1 to 2 tablespoons fresh flat-leaf parsley or cilantro leaves
Guacamole for serving

Directions:

Before you start
Be sure an adult is nearby to help.

Position an oven rack in the middle of an oven and preheat the oven to 450°F.

Build the quesadilla
Using a pastry brush, lightly brush one side of each tortilla with the olive oil. Place 1 tortilla, oiled side down, on a cookie sheet.

Evenly sprinkle the jack cheese over the tortilla. Dollop small amounts of the salsa over the cheese. Top with the herb leaves. Place the second tortilla, oiled side up, on top of the filling.

Cook the quesadilla

Put the cookie sheet in the oven and bake until the top tortilla is lightly browned and crisp looking, 8 to 10 minutes.

Cut the quesadilla

Ask an adult to help you remove the cookie sheet from the oven and place it on a wire cooling rack. Let the quesadilla cool for a couple of minutes.

Next, carefully slide the quesadilla onto a cutting board. Using a pizza cutter or sharp knife, cut the quesadilla into 6 or 8 wedges. Serve immediately, with a small bowl of guacamole for dipping, if you like. Makes 1 quesadilla.

The Ultimate Ham & Cheese

Ingredients:

2 tablespoons unsalted butter
1 tablespoon all-purpose flour
1/2 cup milk
1/4 cup shredded Gruyère cheese
1 pinch of ground nutmeg
Salt and freshly ground pepper, to taste
4 slices sandwich bread
1/4 pound thinly sliced Gruyère cheese
1/4 pound thinly sliced ham

Directions:

Cook butter and flour
Be sure an adult is nearby to help.

Set a small saucepan over medium heat, add 1 tablespoon of the butter and let it melt. Add the flour and cook, whisking constantly, until the mixture has thickened a little and smells nutty, about 1 minute. Do not let it brown.

Make the sauce
Add the milk to the saucepan and whisk very quickly. Reduce the heat to low and cook, stirring constantly with a wooden spoon, until the mixture gets very thick, about 2 minutes. Add the shredded cheese, nutmeg, and a sprinkle each of salt and pepper. Cook, stirring, for 1 minute. Remove the saucepan from the heat.

Build the sandwiches

Lay the bread slices in front of you on a work surface. Using a table knife, divide the cheese sauce between 2 of the slices, spreading it evenly. Layer a slice of cheese, 1 or 2 slices of ham and another slice of cheese on top of the sauce. Top with the remaining bread slices.

Cook the sandwiches

Set a large fry pan over medium heat and add the remaining 1 tablespoon butter. Let it melt, then tilt the fry pan to coat it evenly. Add the sandwiches. Fry until golden brown on one side, about 2 minutes. Use a metal spatula to turn each sandwich and fry the other side, about 2 minutes more. Cut in half and serve immediately. Makes 2 sandwiches.

Dinner

Favorite Spaghetti & Meatballs

Ingredients:

1 garlic clove
1 tablespoon olive oil
1 can (28 ounces) chopped tomatoes
4 teaspoons salt
1 tablespoon oregano
3 tablespoons tomato paste
1 cup water
1 pound ground beef
1 egg
6 saltine crackers, crushed
1/4 teaspoon freshly ground pepper
1 pound spaghetti
Grated Parmesan cheese for serving

Directions:

Chop the garlic
Be sure an adult is nearby to help.

Put the garlic clove on a cutting board. Place the flat part of a metal spatula on top of the garlic clove and press down hard with the heel of your palm to break and loosen the papery skin. Do not worry if you smash the garlic a little.

Peel off the skin and throw it away. Use a knife to cut the garlic into little pieces.

Cook the garlic
Get an adult to help you now. Place a large sauté pan over medium heat. Pour the olive oil into the pan and let it heat for 1 minute.

Add the garlic and stir with a wooden spoon until you can really smell it, about 30 seconds. Do not let it burn!

Make the sauce

Add the tomatoes, 1 teaspoon of the salt, 1 1/2 teaspoons of the oregano, 2 tablespoons of the tomato paste and the 1 cup water to the sauté pan. Stir with the wooden spoon until small bubbles appear on the surface of the sauce. This is called a simmer.

Partially cover the pan with the lid and reduce the heat to low. Let the sauce simmer gently, stirring occasionally, for 15 minutes while you make the meatballs. You will have about 4 cups sauce.

Mix the meatballs

In a large bowl, combine the ground beef, egg, crushed saltine crackers, 1 teaspoon of the salt, the remaining 1 1/2 teaspoons of the oregano, the pepper and the remaining1 tablespoon tomato paste.

Wash and dry your hands thoroughly. Mix and squeeze the mixture with your hands until it is smooth. (Or, you can use the wooden spoon to mix.)

Shape the meatballs

Still using your hands, pluck or scoop a rounded tablespoon of meat from the bowl and roll it between your palms to make a small meatball. Repeat, shaping a total of about 20 small meatballs. As you make the meatballs, set them on a plate.

Wash your hands well before continuing with the recipe.

Cook the meatballs

Turn up the heat under the tomato sauce to medium. Using tongs, carefully put the meatballs into the sauce and cook them gently until they are cooked through, about 10 minutes.

To test whether the meatballs are done, use the tongs to remove one, put it on the cutting board and break it in half. It should be the same grayish color throughout. When the meatballs are done, remove the sauté pan from the heat. Cover to keep warm and set aside.

Cook the spaghetti

Fill a large pot three-quarters full with water. Place over high heat and bring to a rolling boil. When the water is boiling, add the remaining 2 teaspoons salt.

Add the spaghetti to the pot, wait a minute, then stir and push the spaghetti down into the water with a wooden fork. Boil the spaghetti, stirring occasionally to keep it from clumping, until tender but not mushy, about 10 minutes, or according to the instructions on the package.

Put it all together

Set a colander in the sink. Ask an adult to help you pour the spaghetti into the colander. Let the spaghetti drain, shaking the colander a few times to shake off the extra water.

Add the drained spaghetti to the sauce in the sauté pan. Toss until it is well coated with the sauce.

Using the tongs, divide the spaghetti among 4 plates. Add the meatballs, dividing them evenly, then spoon some extra sauce onto each plate of spaghetti. Pass the grated Parmesan cheese at the table. Serves 4.

Sesame Fish Sticks

Ingredients:

1 1/2 pounds halibut, cod or other firm white fish fillets
1 cup all-purpose flour
1/4 teaspoon salt
1/4 teaspoon freshly ground pepper
2 eggs
1 cup sesame seeds
1/4 cup vegetable oil
Lemon wedges for serving
Tartar sauce or tomato ketchup for serving

Directions:

Cut the fish sticks

Before you start, be sure an adult is nearby to help.

Put the fish fillets on a cutting board. Using a sharp knife, cut the fish fillets into sticks measuring about 1 by 5 inches. Transfer to a plate and set aside.

Get ready to coat the fish

Pour the flour into a shallow pan. Sprinkle the salt and pepper over the flour and stir with a fork until blended.

Crack the eggs into another shallow pan, then beat the eggs with the fork until they are smooth and uniformly yellow.

Pour the sesame seeds into a third shallow pan.

Line up the pans of flour, eggs and sesame seeds in a row in front of you, in that order.

Coat the fish sticks

Drag a fish piece through the flour, turning to coat it all over. Gently shake off the extra flour. Now dip the fish piece quickly into the eggs, letting the excess drip off. Finally, drag the fish piece through the sesame seeds, turning it to coat evenly with the seeds. Set it aside on a clean plate. Repeat until you have coated all the fish pieces.

Heat the oil

Place a layer of paper towels on another clean plate.

Get an adult to help you now. Set a sauté pan over medium heat. Pour the oil into the sauté pan and let the oil heat for 1 minute.

Using tongs or a metal spatula, put the fish sticks into the pan, one by one. The coating should sizzle when it touches the oil.

Cook the fish sticks

Put as many fish sticks in the pan as will fit without crowding. There should be a little space around each stick. Cook the fish sticks until golden brown on the first side, about 5 minutes.

Using the tongs or spatula, carefully turn the fish sticks over. Cook the fish sticks on the other side until they are golden, about 5 minutes more.

Keep the fish stick warm

Transfer the fish sticks to the paper towels to drain. Turn the oven to 200°F. Place the first batch of fish sticks in a baking dish. Slide the dish into the oven to keep the fish sticks warm.

Fry the remaining fish sticks and keep them warm in the oven.

Serve it up

Ask an adult to help you remove the fish sticks from the oven. Use the tongs to transfer the fish sticks to a platter.

Serve the fish sticks hot, with lemon wedges for squeezing and tartar sauce or ketchup for dipping. Serves 4.

Lightning Source UK Ltd.
Milton Keynes UK
UKHW052207180722
406035UK00005B/104

9 781681 453880